Yes, I Can LISTEN!

Written by Steve Metzger
Illustrated by Susan Szecsi

Chicago

First edition

Published by Parenting Press

An imprint of Chicago Review Press Incorporated

814 North Franklin Street

Chicago, Illinois 60610

ISBN 978-1-64160-174-0

Library of Congress Cataloging-in-Publication Data

Is available from the Library of Congress.

Printed in the United States of America

5 4 3 2 1

To teachers and librarians around the world . . . who listen to children every day.   — S.M.

To my children Feco and David, my parents, and my husband, Gabor, who have taught me to listen and love.   — S.S.

I Can Listen to My Teachers

I love to go to school each day!
My teachers help me learn

Science, math, and how to read,
and when to take my turn.

I Can Listen to Safety Instructions

It's time for fire safety.
We listen, we're alert.
We hear the bell and go outside,
so no one will get hurt.

I Can Listen to Books

It's story time and I'm all ears!
What is the choice today?

Will we fly to Africa?
Or learn about ballet?

I Can Listen to My Classmates

My friend is very angry.
She wants to tell me why.

My teacher says,
"Please hear her words."

Although it's hard, I try.

I Can Listen to Music

My teacher turns the music on,
I hear the drummer's beat.
A saxophone, a loud guitar,
it's time to move my feet!

I Can Listen to My Parents

When Mommy says, "I love you,"
I feel so warm inside.

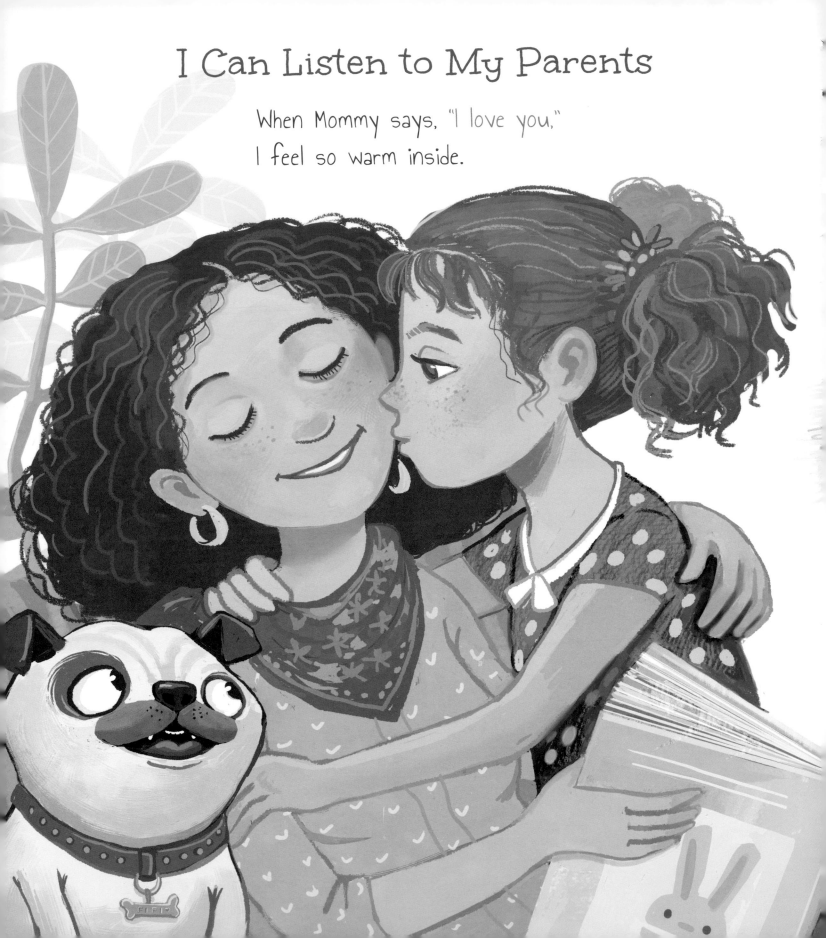

And if I fall, I hear Dad's words,

"It's all right, you tried."

I Can Listen to a Different Point of View

I always like to make the rules
when we go out to play.
But when I hear my friends, I think,
There is another way.

I Can Listen to My Grandparents

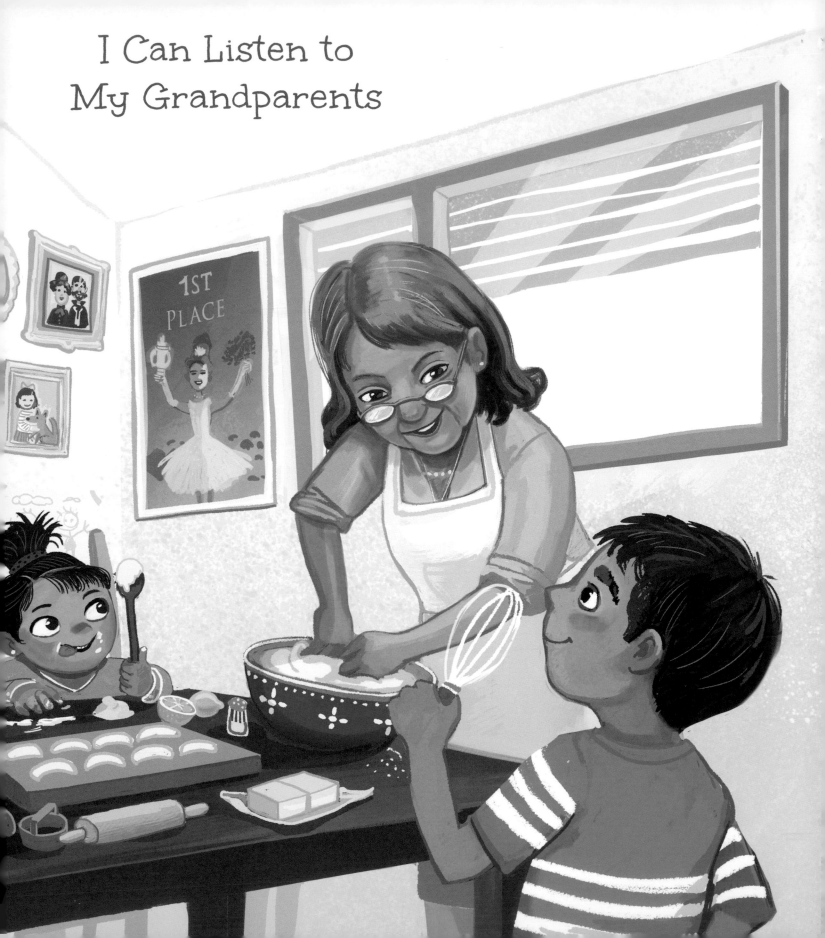

I love Grandma's sweet stories.
She smiles and sounds so wise.

When Grandpa speaks to me
I see a sparkle in his eyes.

I Can Listen to Myself

If I'm upset, I need to find
a quiet place to be.

I take a breath and then find out
what's going on with me.

I Can Listen to Nature

Crunch, crunch, CRUNCH! I love to stomp upon the leafy ground.

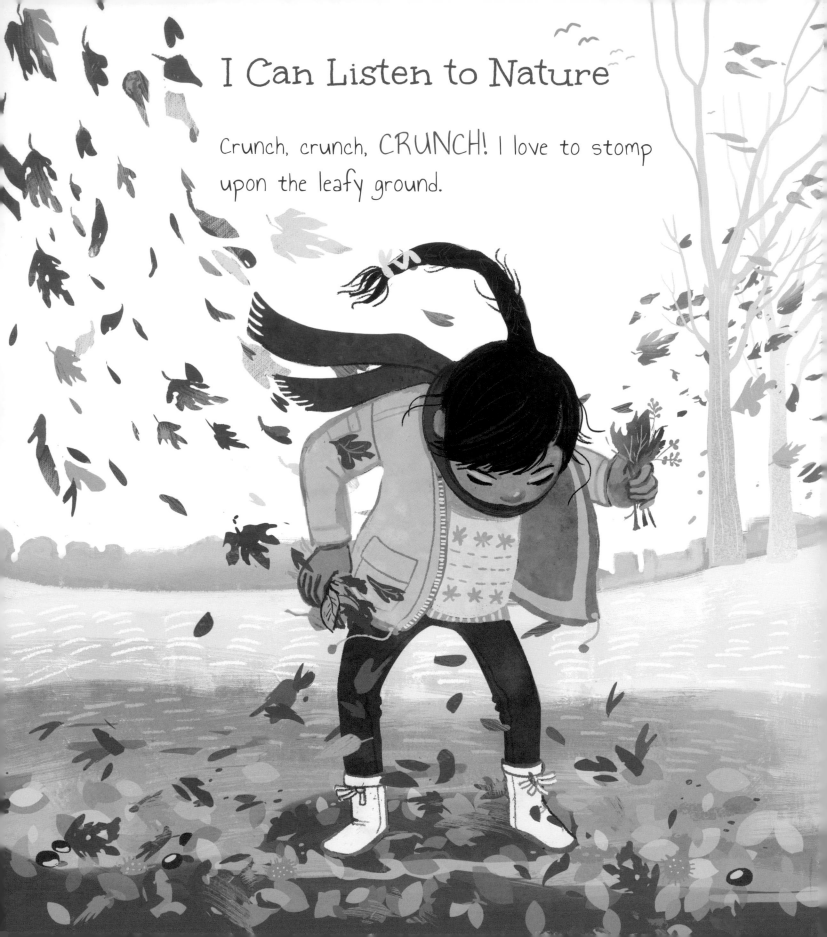

When the wind blows through the trees,
it makes a whooshing sound.

I Can Listen to New Friends

When new children join our class,
we learn their different names.
I like to hear where they came from
and play their favorite games.

Trevor

Zach

Hana

Yasmin

Ethan

Veronica

I Can Listen to Everyday Sounds

A barking dog, a honking horn.
The rain goes pit-a-pat.
A chirping bird that wakes me up.
A gently meowing cat.

Yes, I Can Listen!

When I listen, I can learn,
From books and teachers, too.

Safety rules, a brand-new game,
A different point of view.

A Note to Parents

Listening is an essential life skill that helps your child achieve success at school, follow safety rules, and show others that she or he cares about them. The playful rhymes of Yes, I Can Listen! will encourage your child to appreciate the rewards of attentive listening.

We invite you to consider these suggested activities:

1. Read aloud every day.

Even after children are reading independently, it's still important for them to listen to books on a daily basis. Whether it's after homework or just before bedtime, there's nothing like finding a cozy spot and reading a favorite story or chapter book out loud to your child. Informal discussions about plot development and character motivation help increase comprehension, too.

2. Take a listening walk.

Turn off the electronic devices and go for a walk in the park or around the neighborhood with your child. Being as silent as possible, listen to the sounds of chirping birds, the wind, dogs barking, and children playing. When your walk is over, spend a few moments making a list of everything you just heard. You might be surprised at the variety of sounds.

3. Play a "Follow Directions" game.

Start by asking your child to complete a one-step task, such as, "Lift a cushion over your head." Increase the complexity and fun by adding more and more steps. How many steps can she or he remember? Then invite your child to make up directions for you to follow.

4. Create stories with your family.

Ask family members to sit on chairs arranged in a circle. After one person begins a story, proceed clockwise, taking turns to develop the plot by building on what was just heard. The story continues until someone comes up with an ending. For another way to get started, introduce cards with topics, like "the lost dog" or "a rainy day surprise."

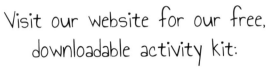

Visit our website for our free,
downloadable activity kit:

www.chicagoreviewpress.com